TIME FOR KIDS READERS

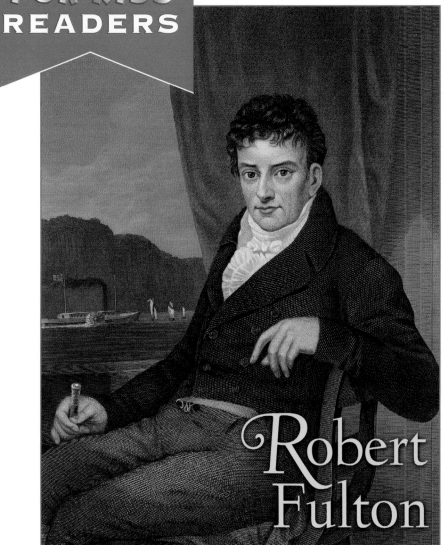

Robert Fulton

by Susan Ring

Harcourt

Orlando   Austin   Chicago   NewYork   Toronto   London   San Diego

Visit *The Learning Site!*
www.harcourtschool.com

Robert Fulton
1765–1815

Robert Fulton was a person who had many ideas. He grew up on a farm in Pennsylvania. As a boy, Robert liked to invent things.

Fulton was born in Lancaster, Pennsylvania. This is how the area once looked.

This scene was painted by the American artist Winslow Homer.

Robert liked to fish with his friends, but he did not like to row the boat. So he made a boat with a paddle wheel. He also made a skyrocket for a town celebration.

Robert Fulton painted this picture of his wife.

Robert liked to paint. When he was 21, he moved to England to learn more about art. He painted a lot, but he still wanted to be an inventor.

In 1797, Fulton had an idea for a boat that could stay underwater. He called his submarine the <u>Nautilus</u>.

Fulton drew these pictures of the <u>Nautilus</u>. He shows the submarine sailing on the water and under the water.

Then Fulton had another idea. He wanted to build a new kind of steamboat. The first steamboat he made sank in the river. But he did not give up on his dream.

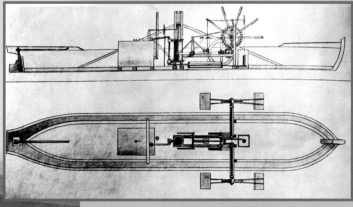

Fulton used his talents both as an artist and an inventor. He drew this plan for an early steamboat.

This is a modern submarine.

Robert Fulton 1804

Many people made fun of the boat. They called it Fulton's Folly. Finally, his dream came true. In 1807, his steamboat made the 150-mile trip up the Hudson River and back.

Because of Robert Fulton, people and goods could now travel to new places much faster.